W9-BGZ-085

ABDO Publishing Company

FISH & GAME
WILD TURKEY

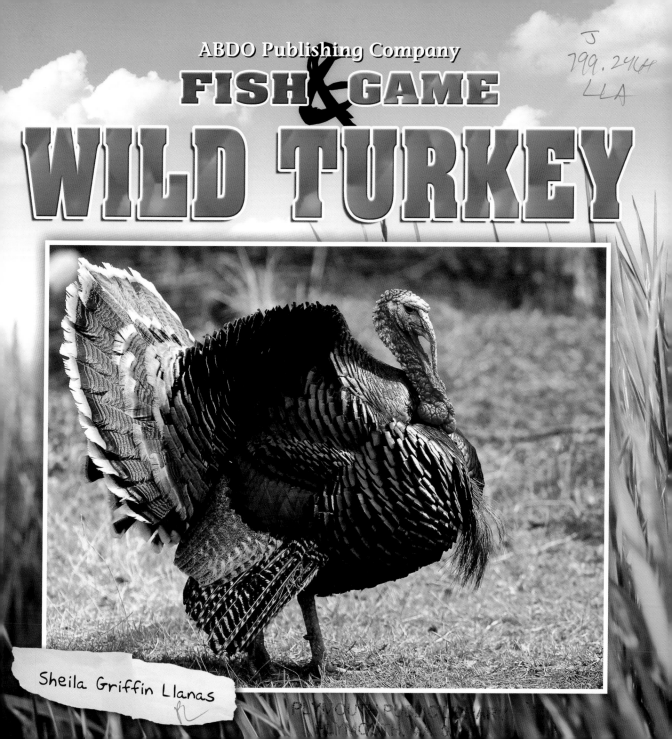

Sheila Griffin Llanas

visit us at
www.abdopublishing.com

Published by ABDO Publishing Company, PO Box 398166, Minneapolis, MN 55439.
Copyright © 2014 by Abdo Consulting Group, Inc. International copyrights reserved in all
countries. No part of this book may be reproduced in any form without written permission from the
publisher. The Checkerboard Library™ is a trademark and logo of ABDO Publishing Company.

Printed in the United States of America, North Mankato, Minnesota.
112013
012014

 PRINTED ON RECYCLED PAPER

Cover Photo: iStockphoto
Interior Photos: Alamy p. 21; AP Images pp. 18–19, 25, 26, 29; Corbis p. 15; Getty Images p. 27;
    Glow Images p. 21; iStockphoto p. 9; JOHN CANCALOSI/National Geographic Creative p.
    13; Library of Congress p. 7; PATRICIO ROBLES GIL/SIERRA MADR/National Geographic
    Creative p. 5; Science Source pp. 11, 16, 25; Thinkstock pp. 1, 23; TIM LAMAN/National
    Geographic Creative p. 12

Editors: Rochelle Baltzer, Megan M. Gunderson, Bridget O'Brien
Art Direction: Neil Klinepier

Library of Congress Cataloging-in-Publication Data

Llanas, Sheila Griffin, 1958-
  Wild turkey / Sheila Griffin Llanas.
       pages cm. -- (Fish & game)
  Includes index.
  Audience: Ages 8-12.
  ISBN 978-1-62403-111-3
  1. Turkey hunting--Juvenile literature. 2. Wild turkey--Juvenile literature. I. Title.
  SK325.T8L57 2014
  799.2'4645--dc23
                              2013034829

Contents

Turkeys!

In the United States, wild turkeys are the second most popular hunting animal after white-tailed deer. And, they are the number one game bird. Hunting them is an American tradition. Each year, about 2.5 million US hunters seek wild turkeys.

Wild turkeys are crafty and secretive. Turkey hunters must be just as crafty! They study wild turkey behaviors and try to outwit the birds. Turkey hunters wear full **camouflage**. They sit very still in the woods and wait for turkeys to appear. Wild turkey hunting takes patience. But, it is an exciting and rewarding outdoor adventure.

Turkeys live in big numbers in the United States. The current wild turkey population may be as high as 7 million! Missouri counts more than 600,000 wild turkeys. Texas has more than 500,000. Alabama and Pennsylvania are each home to more than 350,000.

WILD FACTS!

In French, the wild turkey is a *dindon sauvage*. In Spanish, it is a *guajolote*.

Across the nation, wild turkeys are a valuable natural resource. The birds are native to North America. And they have long been a part of the continent's history.

About 20 percent of US hunters head into the field seeking wild turkeys.

Ancient Bird

    For centuries, Native Americans depended on wild turkeys for meat. The Pueblo people of the Southwest raised turkeys from as early as 200 BCE. They used feathers in ceremonies and to decorate robes. Turkey leg spurs became arrow tips. Leg bones became whistles. Images of turkeys appeared on pottery and rock walls.

    Native Americans knew how to hunt turkeys. They hid near where the birds ate and drank. They imitated turkey calls. When birds drew close, hunters used bows and arrows. Those basic methods are still used today.

    Early European colonists ate wild turkey. It was even present at the first Thanksgiving. But, it was not the central dish like it is today! Founding Father Benjamin Franklin saw the turkey as **uniquely** American. He joked that a turkey would defend the home from British soldiers!

WILD FACTS!

Scientists have found 5 million year old turkey fossils in the United States and Mexico!

In the 1800s, European settlers overhunted wild turkeys for food. Plus, turkeys lost **habitat** when forests were cleared for farms and cities. The wild turkey population shrank. In some states, turkeys disappeared altogether.

Turkey hunting in the 1800s

In Balance

Over time, wild turkeys disappeared from 18 of their original 39 states. By 1851, Massachusetts had no wild turkeys. They were gone from Iowa by 1907. Biologists and farmers tried to revive turkey populations. Yet farm-raised chicks did not survive in the wild.

In the 1950s, conservationists tried a new method. They trapped wild turkeys with nets. They released these birds into areas where turkeys had once lived. Finally, wild turkeys thrived again in US fields and forests.

In 1973, the National Wild Turkey Federation was formed. The organization works to preserve wild turkeys and support hunting. Today, turkey populations have recovered so well the animals can be hunted in every state except Alaska.

Wild turkeys made a remarkable recovery. Today, the nation's wild turkey population is stable and growing. There may be plenty of birds in the fields. But they are not easy to see or find. To hunt wild turkeys, hunters must learn about their biology and behaviors.

Alaska is the only US state that does not have a wild turkey population. Turkeys have even been introduced in Hawaii!

WILD TURKEY TAXONOMY:

Kingdom: Animalia
Phylum: Chordata
Class: Aves
Order: Galliformes
Family: Phasianidae
Subfamily: Meleagridinae
Genus: *Meleagris*
Species: *M. gallopavo*

Snood to Tail

The first thing you might notice about a turkey is its feathers. That's because wild turkeys have 5,000 to 6,000 feathers! Each wing has 10 primary feathers and 18 to 19 secondary feathers. The tail has 18 large **quill** feathers. A turkey's feathers keep it warm and dry.

Wild turkeys have dark-colored feathers. This lets them hide and blend in with fields and woods. Male turkey feathers are red, gold, green, and bronze. They are also **iridescent**. Female feathers are mostly brown, and they are not shiny.

The wild turkey is the largest game bird in North America. Adults have a four-foot (1.2-m) **wingspan**.

Males weigh 10 to 16 pounds (5 to 7 kg). They stand four feet (1.2 m) tall. Females are half that size. They weigh about 6 to 10 pounds (3 to 5 kg) and they have shorter legs. All turkeys have four toes on each foot.

There are six subspecies of Meleagris gallopavo. Easterns (below) are the most common. The other five are Florida, Gould's, Merriam's, Rio Grande, and Mexican wild turkeys.

Male turkeys are called gobblers or toms. Toms have sharp spurs on the backs of their lower legs. These can be 0.5 to 1.5 inches (1.3 to 3.8 cm)

A turkey's tail feathers are usually 12 to 15 inches (30 to 38 cm) long.

long. Males also have beards growing from their chests. These thin beards may look like hair, but they are actually feathers. They can be up to 12 inches (30 cm) long.

Female turkeys are called hens. Hens rarely have beards or spurs.

It takes a dictionary to study the wild turkey's head! Bumps on the tom's head and throat are caruncles. That flap of skin under its chin is a wattle. The fleshy red flap jutting from its beak is a snood. Hens have very small caruncles, wattles, and snoods.

WILD FACTS!

Domestic turkeys are raised for food. They can weigh more than twice as much as wild turkeys.

The Wild Turkey

TAIL

BEAK

EYE

SNOOD

CARUNCLES

WATTLE

BEARD

LEGS

SPURS

FEET

WING

A tom's head can be red, blue, and white. The color changes depending on its mood. A hen has a smaller, blue-gray head.

Hunters must know the difference between hens and toms. To successfully hunt this bird, hunters also need to know all about turkey behaviors.

13

Senses

Wild turkey flocks are organized into a pecking order. That means every animal has its place, with more or less power than others.

To communicate, wild turkeys sound up to 30 calls. One gobble attracts females. Humans can hear this call up to one mile (1.6 km) away! Another call responds to other males. Turkeys cackle as they fly down from roosts. They purr, yelp, and cluck to each other. These noises keep the group together and gather lost members.

Other calls warn of danger, but they cannot always protect turkeys from their natural enemies. Coyotes, eagles, mountain lions, and owls attack adults. Raccoons, skunks, foxes, and opossums go after eggs and chicks. Living with predators has made wild turkeys shy. To stay safe, wild turkeys use extreme caution.

WILD FACTS!

The domestic turkey has a larger body and shorter legs than the wild turkey. So, it has lost the ability to fly.

Wild turkeys can fly up to 55 miles per hour (89 km/h) for as far as a mile.

Turkeys rely on their excellent senses of hearing and sight to avoid danger. Their sense of smell is poor. If danger gets too close, wild turkeys can run up to 25 miles per hour (40 km/h). Or, they can quickly take flight.

Habitat

Wild turkeys live across the United States and in parts of Mexico and southern Canada. To survive, they need two **habitats**. In open fields, they feed and mate. In wooded areas, they roost and hide from predators.

At night, turkeys fly up into branches to sleep. Being high up protects them from ground predators. In early morning, flocks of turkeys come down from their roosting places. They go to clearings, roadsides, open fields, and field edges to feed.

Turkeys have small home ranges.

Gobblers and hens roost separately.

North America

Europe

Asia

Africa

South America

Australia

Where wild turkeys live

N

In winter, they stay in areas of just 50 acres (20 ha). In spring during mating season, they spread out more. But just 640 acres (260 ha) of good land can support a whole flock.

It is important to let turkeys find their own food in the wild. When they enter human **habitats**, they can become territorial. If humans feed them, turkeys may see humans as lower in the pecking order! This can lead to **aggression**.

Time to Eat

Wild turkeys eat what is available. In summer, they **forage** for crop grains, grass seeds, and fruits. In fall, they eat a lot of nuts, such as acorns, beech nuts, hickory nuts, and pecans. In winter, food is more scarce. Then, turkeys may eat fern heads, corn, evergreen ferns, and burdock. Wild turkeys also eat insects, salamanders, snails, and beetles.

Turkeys mainly peck the ground to eat. They

WILD FACTS!

Besides a flock, a group of turkeys may be called a rafter. A flock often contains up to 30 turkeys. In winter, it may number more than 200!

use their strong feet to scratch leaves out of the way. And, they are strong enough to dig up plant bulbs. If they need to, turkeys fly up into bushes or trees to find food.

Turkeys have a crop, which is a cavity where food is stored. The crop allows turkeys to eat faster than they can **digest**. They can eat up to one pound (0.5 kg) of food at a single meal.

Wild turkeys usually eat for two to three hours after dawn and before dusk.

Turkeys swallow foods whole. In the crop, food is softened. Then it enters the gizzard. This muscular stomach chamber grinds food. It can grind up hard nuts, such as wild pecans, in an hour. Harder foods, such as hickory nuts, can take up to 30 hours.

Life Cycle

   In early spring, toms put on a show to attract hens. They gobble, fan their tails, and puff their feathers. Toms strut, drag their wings, and make drumming sounds.

   After mating, hens hollow out shallow nests in the ground. They use nearby leaves or other material to line them. Gobblers have no fatherly duties.

   Hens lay one egg a day until there are 4 to 17 eggs. Then, they **incubate** the eggs for about 28 days.

   Young turkeys are called chicks or poults. Females are called jennies. Males are called jakes.

   Poults grow fast! They can walk and feed themselves within 24 hours. They eat lots of insects, which provide protein for growing. They also eat berries and seeds. By three weeks, poults can fly up into roosts.

   Young chicks are covered with tan, brown, pink, and gray **down**. Their dark legs will turn pink as they age. A jake has a short beard and just a few long middle tail feathers. As a tom, its tail feathers will all be the same length.

Poults must work hard to survive. Wild turkeys have short lives. On average, they live only three years. The oldest on record lived 13 years.

Wild turkey eggs are pale yellowish tan with reddish brown or pinkish spots. Eggs measure about 1.9 to 2.7 inches (4.9 to 6.9 cm) long.

Jakes stay near their mother until fall. Jennies stay until the following spring.

Legal Hunts

It is helpful for hunters to know the life cycle of the wild turkey. Many states offer two hunting seasons, one in spring and one in fall.

Hunting experiences can be pretty different. For example, the spring season may be shorter and only gobblers may be hunted legally. To protect the species, hens must be allowed to lay and **incubate** eggs.

The fall season can be more challenging. Turkeys move more and call less than during the spring mating season. Hens are done raising chicks. So, some states allow hunters to get both hens and toms.

Spring and fall hunting dates and times vary from state to state. Check the calendar and watch the clock. It's up to each hunter to learn and follow the rules. Luckily, most states offer a remarkable amount of hunting information online.

WILD FACTS!

In 2012, Minnesota issued 42,817 turkey permits. Of those, 8,664 were youth permits!

Responsible hunters observe turkeys to make certain they can tell hens and gobblers apart.

For many hunters, turkey hunting is an annual tradition. Before heading out, turkey hunters apply for state licenses. They get permits, tags, and anything else required for where they plan to hunt. Some states limit the number of permits issued. This prevents overhunting. Others limit hunting to archery only for part of the season.

Preseason

To find wild turkeys, hunters often scout hunting areas before the season starts. They look for turkey signs, such as feathers, scratch marks in the dirt, and droppings. Gobbler droppings are shaped like the letter *J*. Hen droppings are curled up in a spiral. The older the turkey, the larger the droppings.

Preseason, hunters also gather equipment from wardrobe to weapons. In full **camouflage** clothing, hunters blend in with the woods. Keen-eyed turkeys can't see them. But for safety, hunters must make their presence known to other hunters. Some states require hunters to wear blaze orange for this reason.

The right shotgun must be easy for the hunter to carry, lift, and aim. A 20-**gauge** shotgun is popular for turkey hunting. So is a 12-gauge. No matter what the choice, firearms must be registered and legal.

Hunting is always a safety-first sport. Hunter training and understanding of weapons safety are key. Before taking aim, a hunter must be certain of his or her target and what is beyond it. He or she must keep the finger away from the trigger until ready to shoot. Guns must be unloaded when not in use. And, they must always be pointed in a safe direction.

Camouflage may even disguise a turkey hunter's gun.

Tom tracks measure 6 to 7 inches (15 to 18 cm) long.
Hen tracks are shorter at 4.5 to 5 inches (11 to 13 cm) long.

Game Time

Hunters must get these cautious birds to come to them. They trick a shy tom into coming close by making him curious. Two helpful tools attract wild turkeys. One is the turkey call. The other is the **decoy**.

Some hunters make animal calls with their own voices. Others use tools purchased from hunting stores.

The spring hunt is all about gobbling. Toms gobble a lot in spring. They are looking for hens! Hunters may make the sound of a hen to lure a tom out of hiding. Or, they may make the sound of a predator owl, crow, or coyote. Sometimes, toms gobble out a warning response. This way, the hunter gets the turkey's general location.

Hunters never call too often. It makes suspicious gobblers grow quiet. Turkeys don't like to reveal their location to enemies. Hunters are careful for another reason, too. They want to fool turkeys, not other hunters. Accidents happen when turkey hunters fail to identify their target. They mistake a person for a turkey.

The other important tool is the **decoy**. Hunters set out plastic turkeys. Curious gobblers might come out of hiding to investigate.

Decoys may look like male or female turkeys.

Hunters are most successful when a bird comes within 40 yards (37 m). Hunters aim for a turkey's most vulnerable areas, the head and the neck. If they are successful, it's time to clean the bird and head home.

Day's End

  After a successful hunt, responsible hunters follow state regulations for registering their bird. Rules vary by state. They may require that the bird be tagged, with information such as name and license number included. Often, the tag must be attached to the turkey's leg. That way, officials can tell whether it is a hen or a tom.

  Some people eat wild turkey. Others want to display their trophy. They will take the bird to a **taxidermist**. In either case, the animal must be handled with care.

  Field dressing a turkey requires skill and an adult's help. Wear plastic gloves. With the bird on its back, cut open the belly. Carefully remove the entrails. Do not cut the crop, stomach, or intestines. They contain harmful bacteria. Rinse the body cavity in clean water and place a bag of ice inside. Wipe the bird clean and dry. Wrap up the meat and store it in a cooler.

Before heading home, double-check that all firearms are unloaded. Wear blaze orange clothing to walk out of the woods. Cover the turkey with blaze orange, too. Walk on a clearly marked path. These practices help prevent other hunters from mistaking a person for wildlife.

Turkey hunting is a tradition passed down from one generation to the next.

At home, clean and safely store shotguns or bows and arrows. Clean and put away **camouflage** clothing. The gear will need to be in top shape for the next turkey season! Wild turkeys are a valuable American game bird. They are part of the nation's hunting tradition.

Glossary

aggression (uh-GREH-shuhn) - forceful or hostile actions.

camouflage (KA-muh-flahzh) - a disguise or way of hiding something by covering it up or changing its appearance.

decoy - a fake bird used to lure real birds within shooting distance of humans.

digest - to break down food into simpler substances the body can absorb.

down - soft, fluffy feathers.

field dressing - the task of removing an animal's internal organs after it has been taken by a hunter.

forage - to search.

gauge - a measurement relating to ammunition or the distance across a gun barrel.

habitat - a place where a living thing is naturally found.

incubate - to keep eggs warm, often by sitting on them, so they will hatch.

iridescent (ihr-uh-DEH-suhnt) - shining with many colors when seen from different angles.

quill - a large, stiff feather or a sharp spine.

taxidermist - someone who prepares, stuffs, and mounts the skins of dead animals so that the animals look like they did when they were alive.

uniquely (yoo-NEEK-lee) - in a way that makes something one of a kind.

wingspan - the distance from one wing tip to the other when the wings are spread.

To learn more about wild turkeys, visit ABDO Publishing Company online. Web sites about wild turkeys are listed on our Book Links page. These links are routinely monitored and updated to provide the most current information available.

www.abdopublishing.com

Index

B
beak 12
beard 12, 21
bows and arrows 6, 23, 29

C
calls 6, 14, 22, 26, 27
camouflage 4, 24, 29
Canada 16
caruncles 12
color 10, 13, 20
communication 14, 20
crop 19

D
decoys 26, 27
defenses 10, 14, 15, 16, 26
diet 16, 18, 19, 20
droppings 24

E
eggs 14, 20, 22

F
feathers 6, 10, 12, 20, 21, 24
feet 11, 19
field dressing 27, 28
firearms 24, 25, 29
flocks 14, 16, 17
flying 14, 15, 16, 19, 20

G
gizzard 19

H
habitat 7, 16, 17
head 12, 13, 27
history 6, 7, 8
home range 16, 17
hunting 4, 6, 8, 9, 13, 22, 23, 24, 25, 26, 27, 28, 29

L
legs 6, 11, 12, 20, 28
license 23, 28
life span 21

M
Mexico 16

N
National Wild Turkey Federation 8
nest 20

P
pecking order 14, 17
permit 23
population 4, 7, 8, 9
poults 8, 14, 20, 21, 22
predators 14, 16, 26

R
reproduction 16, 20, 22, 26
roost 14, 16, 20
running 15

S
safety 24, 25, 27, 29
scratch marks 24
senses 15, 24
size 10, 11, 12
snood 12
spurs 6, 12

T
tag 23, 28
tail 10, 20, 21
taxidermy 28
Thanksgiving 6
threats 7, 8, 21, 23
toes 11

U
United States 4, 5, 7, 8, 16

W
wattle 12
wings 10, 20